TiGeRS ROaR!

Pam Scheunemann

Consulting Editor, Diane Craig, M.A./Reading Specialist

ABDO
Publishing Company

Published by ABDO Publishing Company, 8000 West 78th Street, Edina, Minnesota 55439.

Printed in the United States.

Editor: Katherine Hengel
Content Developer: Nancy Tuminelly
Cover and Interior Design and Production: Oona Gaarder-Juntti, Mighty Media
Photo Credits: AbleStock, ShutterStock

Library of Congress Cataloging-in-Publication Data

Scheunemann, Pam, 1955-
  Tigers roar! / Pam Scheunemann.
    p. cm. -- (Animal sounds)
  ISBN 978-1-60453-572-3
  1. Tigers--Juvenile literature. I. Title.

QL737.C23S335 2009
599.756--dc22

                        2008033922

SandCastle™ Level: Transitional

SandCastle™ books are created by a team of professional educators, reading specialists, and content developers around five essential components—phonemic awareness, phonics, vocabulary, text comprehension, and fluency—to assist young readers as they develop reading skills and strategies and increase their general knowledge. All books are written, reviewed, and leveled for guided reading, early reading intervention, and Accelerated Reader® programs for use in shared, guided, and independent reading and writing activities to support a balanced approach to literacy instruction. The SandCastle™ series has four levels that correspond to early literacy development. The levels are provided to help teachers and parents select appropriate books for young readers.

Emerging Readers
(no flags)

Beginning Readers
(1 flag)

Transitional Readers
(2 flags)

Fluent Readers
(3 flags)

SandCastle™ would like to hear from you. Please send us your comments and suggestions.
sandcastle@abdopublishing.com

The tiger has a very loud roar.

Tigers, lions, leopards, and jaguars are the only cats that can roar.

It can eat and eat
and eat some more.

It is possible for these big cats
to eat 60 pounds (27 kg) of food
in one night.

Tiger cubs like to play.

Tiger cubs weigh just over two pounds (1 kg) at birth.

Tigers sleep for most of the day.

Tigers are nocturnal. They are most active at night.

Tiger stripes are very nice.

Their stripes provide camouflage in tall grass. This helps tigers sneak up on their prey.

The pattern is never repeated twice!

Each tiger has a unique
pattern of stripes.

Tigers eat mostly meat.

Tigers hunt antelope, deer, wild pigs, and other large mammals.

To see them swim
is a treat!

Tigers are one of the only cats that like to swim!

Tigers have very big paws.

The soft pads on their paws help them walk quietly while hunting.

When they walk, they pull in their claws.

Tigers retract their claws when they aren't using them. This keeps their claws sharp.

When you hear
a tiger roar,
it's a sound you
can't ignore!

A tiger's roar can be heard
up to 2 miles (3 km) away.

Glossary

camouflage (p. 11) – being hidden from sight by use of a disguise or protective coloring that blends into the surrounding environment.

ignore (p. 23) – to not pay attention to someone or something.

imitate (p. 24) – to copy or mimic someone or something.

mammal (p. 15) – a warm-blooded animal that is covered with hair and, in the female, produces milk to feed the young.

pattern (pp. 12, 13) – one or more things that repeat in a recognizable way.

prey (p. 11) – an animal that is hunted by another animal.

retract (p. 20) – to pull back in.

unique (p. 13) – the only one of its kind.

Animal Sounds Around the World

Tigers sound the same no matter where they live. But the way that humans imitate them depends on what language they speak. Here are some examples of how people around the world make tiger sounds:

English - raa   **French** - grr
German - grr   **Greek** - grr
Japanese - gaooooo   **Spanish** - grrr

To see a complete list of SandCastle™ books and other nonfiction titles from ABDO Publishing Company, visit **www.abdopublishing.com**.

8000 West 78th Street, Edina, MN 55439 • 800-800-1312 • fax 952-831-1632